cloverleaf books™

Our American Symbols

Can You Sing "The Star-Spangled Banner"?

Martha E. H. Rustad

illustrated by Kyle Poling

M MILLBROOK PRESS • MINNEAPOLIS

For Maurya —M.E.H.R.

For Dad and Mom, Joanne and
Herman, Donna and Ned, and Eva
Jean and Jim
                      —K.P.

Millbrook Press
A division of Lerner Publishing Group, Inc.
241 First Avenue North
Minneapolis, MN 55401 USA

For reading levels and more information, look up this title at
www.lernerbooks.com.

Main body text set in Slappy Inline 18/28.
Typeface provided by T26.

Library of Congress Cataloging-in-Publication Data

Rustad, Martha E. H. (Martha Elizabeth Hillman), 1975–
      Can you sing "The Star-Spangled Banner"? / by Martha E.
  H. Rustad ; Illustrated by Kyle Poling.
        pages   cm. — (Cloverleaf Books™ — Our American
  Symbols)
      Includes index.
      ISBN 978-1-4677-2136-3 (lib. bdg. : alk. paper)
      ISBN 978-1-4677-4770-7 (eBook)
      1. Baltimore, Battle of, Baltimore, Md., 1814—Juvenile
  literature. 2. Star-spangled banner (Song)—Juvenile literature.
  3. Key, Francis Scott, 1779–1843—Juvenile literature. I. Poling,
  Kyle. II. Title.
  E356.B2R86 2015
  973.5'230975271—dc23   2013046479

Manufactured in the United States of America
1 – BP – 7/15/14

TABLE OF CONTENTS

The Star-Spangled Banner

Oh,   say   can   you   see   by   the dawn's ear - ly   light

What so proud - ly   we   hailed   at the twi - light's last gleam - ing,

the per - il - ous   fight

Chapter One
A Patriotic Song

Time for music class!

Ms. Hill says, "Today we will sing our **national anthem.** That's our country's **patriotic** song."

"I forget what *patriotic* means," says Sanjay.

Many other countries have national anthems. Canada's is called "O Canada." In Great Britain, people sing "God Save the Queen." Japan's anthem is called "Kimigayo."

"It means 'proud of our country,'" Ms. Hill tells us. "Our national anthem is called **'The Star-Spangled Banner.'** It is about the United States flag."

Ms. Hill plays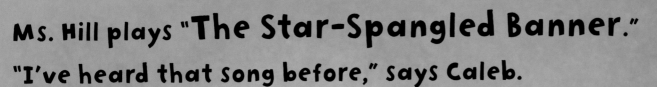

"I've heard that song before," says Caleb.

"Yes, right before our soccer game!" says DeAnna.

"People often sing it before games and other events," says our music teacher.

We learn that during the song, people stand up and look at the flag. They take off their hats and put their hand on their hearts.

"But why?" asks Eva.

"We show **respect** during 'The Star-Spangled Banner' in order to show respect to our country," Ms. Hill says.

The US flag and "The Star-Spangled Banner" are both symbols of the United States. A symbol is something that stands for something else.

Chapter Two

A War Poem

We learn a poet named **Francis Scott Key** wrote the words to our national anthem during a battle in 1814. The United States and Great Britain were fighting a war.

"Was that the Revolutionary War?" asks Zane.

"No, this was the **War of 1812**," says our music teacher.

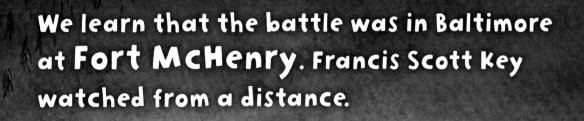

We learn that the battle was in Baltimore at **Fort McHenry**. Francis Scott Key watched from a distance.

The United States of America was only thirty-six years old when the War of 1812 began. During the war, British soldiers burned buildings in Washington, DC. One of them was the White House!

"But what are all those big words?" asks Gerald.

"Let's look closely at them," says Ms. Hill. Yolanda reads

Oh, say can you see by the dawn's early light

What so proudly we hailed at the twilight's last gleaming,

"What does *dawn* mean?" asks our music teacher.

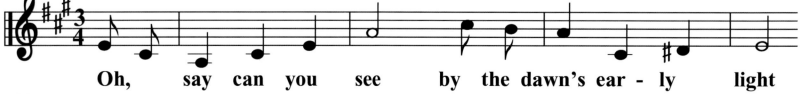

10

When Mr. Key wrote "we hailed," he meant "we saw," or "we pointed out." The word *gleaming* means "shining." The "twilight's last gleaming" is the last bit of sunshine before the dark of night.

"Early morning!" says Hannah.

"Yes. And twilight is after sunset," says Ms. Hill.

"The writer was trying to see something in the dark."

What so proud-ly we hailed at the twi-light's last gleam-ing,

Ms. Hill reads the next lines.

Whose broad stripes and bright stars through the perilous fight

O'er the ramparts we watched were so gallantly streaming?

"What has stripes and stars?" asks our music teacher.

"Our flag!" we all say.

"*Perilous* means 'dangerous,'" Ms. Hill says. "A dangerous battle was going on. A **rampart** is a fort wall. Mr. Key was waiting to see which flag flew over the fort."

Mary Pickersgill sewed the huge flag that flew over Fort McHenry. It was 30 feet (9 meters) wide and 42 feet (13 meters) long. in 1814, our country had fifteen states. So the flag had fifteen stars and fifteen stripes.

Whose broad stripes and bright   stars   through the   per - il - ous   fight

Nyla asks, "Why does it matter which flag was there?"
"The winners of a battle flew their flag," our teacher says.
"When Mr. Key saw the American flag, he knew the
United States had won the battle."

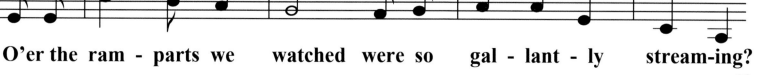

O'er the ram - parts we   watched   were so   gal - lant - ly   stream-ing?

Jamil reads the next lines.

And the rockets' red glare, the bombs bursting in air,
Gave proof through the night that our flag was still there.
"The rockets and bombs lit up the night sky," says Ms. Hill.

The poem by Francis Scott Key has four parts, which are called verses. We sing only the first verse in our national anthem.

And the rock - ets' red glare, the bombs burst - ing in air,

"Like fireworks?" asks Torie.

"Just like fireworks," our music teacher answers.

"Mr. Key saw the huge American flag by that light.

He knew we had won the battle."

Gave   proof through the night   that our   flag   was   still   there.

"Let's read the last lines together," says Ms. Hill.

> Oh, say does that star-spangled banner yet wave
> O'er the land of the free and the home of the brave?

"What is the star-spangled banner?" she asks.

"Our flag!" we all say.

"Right," says our music teacher.

Oh,   say does that   star - spangled   banner   yet   wave

The tune for "The Star-Spangled Banner" comes from an English song called "To Anacreon in Heaven" written by John Stafford Smith.

"Mr. Key also says Americans are free and brave. What does *brave* mean to you?"

"I have to be brave when I go to the dentist," says Olive.

"My cousin is brave. He is in the army," Jenny says.

O'er the land of the free and the home of the brave?

Chapter Three

Our National Anthem

"Why do we sing the national anthem?" asks Pauline.

"Good question. Let's think about it," says Ms. Hill.

"What do we sing on someone's birthday?"

"Happy Birthday!" we all say.

Our music teacher says, "Right! We sing 'Happy Birthday' to celebrate you. We sing the national anthem to celebrate our country."

Some Americans wanted a different song to be our national anthem. They thought "Yankee Doodle Dandy" or "America the Beautiful" would be a better choice.

We learn that in 1814, the United States was a young country. Singing the song helped bring Americans together.

"Francis Scott Key was inspired to write the national anthem as he watched the battle at Fort McHenry," says Ms. Hill. "*Inspired* means 'to have a good idea.' What inspires you?"

"Music inspires me to dance," says Rena.

Tomás says, "My brother laughs at my jokes. He inspires me to make up new ones."

US leaders picked "The Star-Spangled Banner" as our national anthem in 1931.

SCHOOL

Music class is done.

We say, "Thank you, Ms. Hill. See you next week!"

It's time for recess. We stop before our kickball game.

Together we sing the national anthem. Game time!

Write a Patriotic Poem

"The Star-Spangled Banner" is a poem that celebrates the United States of America. You can write a poem that celebrates our country. In an acrostic poem, the first letters of each line spell a word or a name.

What you need:
paper
pencil

1) Choose one of these words:
   STAR, FLAG, AMERICA, BANNER,
   ANTHEM, FREE, BRAVE.

   On your paper, write the word going down,
   with one letter on each line.

2) Think about our country.
   What makes you think of America?
   What are some symbols of the United States?
   What are you most thankful for in our country?

3) Put one patriotic thought or idea on each line.
   The first word of each line will start with a letter
   from the word that you chose in step 1.

4) Share your poem with your friends and family.
   You could even sing it!

Shining bursts of fireworks
Touch the sky
And I am free like the
Raining sparks.

GLOSSARY

anthem: a song that celebrates a country

banner: a flag

celebrate: to do something to show how special or important a day is

dawn: the first sunlight in the morning

gallantly: bravely

gleaming: shining brightly

government: a group of people who make rules for a country

hailed: saw or pointed out

inspired: to have a great idea

patriotic: to be proud of a country

perilous: dangerous

rampart: a thick wall around a fort

respect: to admire or have a good opinion of something or someone

streaming: floating or waving in the wind

symbol: something that stands for something else

tune: a song

twilight: the last sunlight before night

BOOKS

Kulling, Monica. *Francis Scott Key's Star-Spangled Banner.* New York: Random House Children's Books, 2012.
Find out more about the author of "The Star-Spangled Banner" and his poem.

Landau, Elaine. *The National Anthem.* New York: Children's Press, 2008.
Read more about how Francis Scott Key came to write "The Star-Spangled Banner."

Rustad, Martha E. H. *Why Are There Stripes on the American Flag?* Minneapolis: Millbrook Press, 2015.
Learn about the history of the US flag, why the flag is a symbol of freedom, and why we say the Pledge of Allegiance as a show of respect.

WEBSITES

Fort McHenry
http://www.nps.gov/fomc/index.htm
Visit the fort where our national anthem was written.

The Star-Spangled Banner
http://amhistory.si.edu/starspangledbanner/
Learn the story behind the flag that inspired our national anthem.

Symbols of the U.S. Government
http://bensguide.gpo.gov/k-2/symbols/anthem.html
This website from the U.S. Government Printing Office tells about famous symbols of the government of the United States.

LERNER *e* SOURCE™
Expand learning beyond the printed book. Download free, complementary educational resources for this book from our website, www.lerneresource.com.

INDEX